I0455267

August 2013

DOD FINANCIAL MANAGEMENT

Ineffective Risk Management Could Impair Progress toward Audit-Ready Financial Statements

GAO-13-123

August 2013

DOD FINANCIAL MANAGEMENT

Ineffective Risk Management Could Impair Progress toward Audit-Ready Financial Statements

Why GAO Did This Study

The National Defense Authorization Act (NDAA) of Fiscal Year 2010 mandated that DOD's consolidated financial statements be validated as audit ready by September 30, 2017. The NDAA for Fiscal Year 2012 further mandated that DOD's General Fund Statement of Budgetary Resources be audit ready by the end of fiscal year 2014. DOD issued the FIAR Plan and related guidance to provide a strategy and methodology for achieving its audit readiness goals. However, substantial risks exist that may impede DOD's ability to implement the FIAR methodology and achieve audit readiness.

GAO was asked to assess DOD's risk management process for implementing its FIAR Plan. This report addresses the extent to which DOD has established an effective process for identifying, analyzing, and mitigating risks that could impede its progress in achieving audit readiness. GAO interviewed DOD and component officials, reviewed relevant documentation, and compared DOD's risk management processes with guiding principles for risk management.

What GAO Recommends

GAO recommends that DOD design and implement policies and procedures for FIAR Plan risk management that fully incorporate the five risk management guiding principles and consider the Navy's and DLA's risk management practices. While DOD did not fully concur, it cited planned actions that are consistent with GAO's recommendations and findings. These are good first steps, but GAO believes additional action is warranted. GAO affirms its recommendations.

View GAO-13-123. For more information, contact Asif A. Khan at (202) 512-9869 or khana@gao.gov

What GAO Found

The Department of Defense (DOD) has taken some actions to manage its department-level risks associated with preparing auditable financial statements through its Financial Improvement and Audit Readiness (FIAR) Plan. However, its actions were not fully in accordance with widely recognized guiding principles for effective risk management, which include (1) identifying risks that could prevent it from achieving its goals, (2) assessing the magnitude of those risks, (3) developing risk mitigation plans, (4) implementing mitigating actions to address the risks, and (5) monitoring the effectiveness of those mitigating actions. DOD did not have documented policies and procedures for following these guiding principles to effectively manage risks to the implementation of the FIAR Plan.

In January 2012, DOD identified six departmentwide risks to FIAR Plan implementation: lack of DOD-wide commitment, insufficient accountability, poorly defined scope and requirements, unqualified or inexperienced personnel, insufficient funding, and information system control weaknesses. DOD officials stated that risks are discussed on an ongoing basis during various FIAR oversight committee meetings; however, the risks they initially identified were not comprehensive, and they did not provide evidence of efforts to identify additional risks. For example, based on prior audits, GAO identified other audit-readiness risks that DOD did not identify, such as the reliance on service providers for much of the components' financial data and the need for better department-wide document retention policies. Risk management guiding principles provide that risk identification is an iterative process in which new risks may evolve or become known as a program progresses throughout its life cycle.

Similarly, DOD's actions to manage its identified risks were not in accordance with the guiding principles. GAO found little evidence that DOD analyzed risks it identified to assess their magnitude or that DOD developed adequate plans for mitigating the risks. DOD's risk mitigation plans, published in its FIAR Plan Status Reports, consisted of brief, high-level summaries that did not include critical management information, such as specific and detailed plans for implementation, assignment of responsibility, milestones, or resource needs. In addition, information about DOD's mitigation efforts was not sufficient for DOD to monitor the extent of progress in mitigating identified risks.

Without effective risk management at the department-wide level to help ensure the success of the FIAR Plan implementation, DOD is at increased risk of not achieving audit readiness initially for its Statement of Budgetary Resources and ultimately for its complete set of financial statements.

GAO identified two DOD components—the Navy and the Defense Logistics Agency (DLA)—that had established practices consistent with risk management guiding principles, such as preparing risk registers, employing analytical techniques to assess risk, and engaging internal and external stakeholders consistently to assess and identify new risks. These components' actions could serve as a starting point for improving department-level risk management.

Contents

Abbreviations

CMO	Chief Management Officer
CPA	certified public accountant
DCMO	Deputy Chief Management Officer
DFAS	Defense Finance and Accounting Service
DLA	Defense Logistics Agency
DOD	Department of Defense
ERP	enterprise resource planning
FIAR	Financial Improvement and Audit Readiness
FISCAM	*Federal Information System Controls Audit Manual*
FMR	Financial Management Regulation
IG	Inspector General
NARA	National Archives and Records Administration
NDAA	National Defense Authorization Act
OIG	Office of Inspector General
SBR	Statement of Budgetary Resources
SSAE	Statement on Standards for Attestation Engagements

GAO U.S. GOVERNMENT ACCOUNTABILITY OFFICE

441 G St. N.W.
Washington, DC 20548

August 2, 2013

The Honorable Thomas R. Carper
Chairman
The Honorable Tom Coburn
Ranking Member
Committee on Homeland Security and Governmental Affairs
United States Senate

The Honorable Claire McCaskill
Chairman
Subcommittee on Financial and Contracting Oversight
Committee on Homeland Security and Governmental Affairs
United States Senate

The Department of Defense (DOD) has had serious problems with its financial management operations for decades. Pervasive financial management, business operations, and systems weaknesses have adversely affected DOD's ability to control costs; ensure basic accountability; anticipate future claims and costs on the budget (such as health care, weapons systems, and active duty payroll); measure performance; maintain control of funds; prevent and detect fraud, waste, and abuse; address pressing management issues; and prepare auditable financial statements.

Since 1995, DOD financial management has been on GAO's list of programs and operations at high risk of fraud, waste, abuse, and mismanagement.[1] Previous attempts at reform have largely proven unsuccessful, including repeated attempts since fiscal year 1996 to achieve auditability. DOD remains the only major federal agency that has been unable to receive an audit opinion of any kind on its department-wide financial statements. Given the size and complexity of DOD's worldwide operations—involving a requested budget of approximately $614 billion for fiscal year 2013—accurate, complete, and timely financial management information and effective accountability are critical.

Overhauling DOD's financial management presents a major management challenge that goes far beyond financial statement auditability to

---

[1] GAO, *High-Risk Series: An Update*, GAO-13-283 (Washington, D.C.: February 2013).

transforming DOD's business processes and operations. The successful transformation of DOD's business processes and operations will allow DOD to routinely generate timely, complete, and reliable financial and other information for day-to-day management decision making, including resource allocation decisions. Auditable financial statements should be a natural by-product of the ability to produce reliable financial information.

To encourage progress, the National Defense Authorization Act (NDAA) for Fiscal Year 2010 mandated that DOD develop and maintain a Financial Improvement and Audit Readiness (FIAR) Plan that among other things, describes the specific actions to be taken and costs associated with ensuring that its department-wide financial statements are validated as audit ready by September 30, 2017.[2] In October 2011, the Secretary of Defense directed the department to accelerate audit readiness for key elements of its financial statements. Subsequently, the NDAA for Fiscal Year 2013 amended this requirement to add that the FIAR Plan should also support the goal of validating audit readiness of the department's Statement of Budgetary Resources (SBR) no later than September 30, 2014.[3]

As we have previously reported, DOD has developed a methodology to implement the FIAR Plan—issued as the FIAR Guidance—which is reasonable and, if implemented as intended, should enable the department to identify and address its financial management weaknesses and thereby achieve auditability.[4] However, we have also reported on concerns with the department's efforts to implement this methodology. For example, our review of the Navy's Civilian Pay and Air Force's

---

[2] As described in the FIAR Guidance, validation of audit readiness occurs when the DOD Comptroller examines a DOD component's documentation supporting its assertion of audit readiness and concurs with the assertion. This takes place after the DOD Comptroller or independent auditor first reviews the documentation and agrees that it supports audit readiness. A component asserts audit readiness when it believes that its documentation and internal controls are sufficient to support a financial statement audit that will result in an audit opinion. National Defense Authorization Act for Fiscal Year 2010, Pub. L. No. 111-84, § 1003(a), (b), 123 Stat. 2190, 2439-40 (Oct. 28, 2009).

[3] The SBR provides information about budgetary resources made available to an agency as well as the status of those resources at a specific point in time. National Defense Authorization Act for 2013, Pub. L. No. 112-239, §1005, (a) (Jan. 2, 2013).

[4] GAO, *Department of Defense: Financial Management Improvement and Audit Readiness Efforts Continue to Evolve*, GAO-10-1059T (Washington, D.C.: Sept. 29, 2010), and *DOD Financial Management: Improvement Needed in DOD Components' Implementation Audit Readiness Effort*, GAO-11-851 (Washington, D.C.: Sept. 13, 2011).

GAO-13-123 DOD Financial Management

Military Equipment audit readiness efforts identified significant deficiencies in the components' execution of the FIAR Guidance, resulting in insufficient testing and unsupported conclusions.[5]

Objective, Scope, and Methodology

Given DOD's difficulties in achieving audit readiness and addressing its long-standing financial management deficiencies, you asked us to assess DOD's risk management process for implementing its FIAR Plan. Our objective was to determine the extent to which DOD has established an effective process for identifying, analyzing, and addressing risks that could impede its progress in achieving audit readiness.

To address this objective, we identified relevant guiding principles and leading practices of risk management used by the private sector and GAO.[6] Based on our analysis, we found commonalities and identified five basic guiding principles governing effective risk management: (1) identify risks, (2) analyze risks, (3) plan for risk mitigation, (4) implement a risk mitigation plan, and (5) monitor risks and mitigation plans. Using these guiding principles as criteria, we analyzed DOD documents related to risk management, such as the May 2012 and November 2012 FIAR Plan Status Reports,[7] which identified DOD's program risks and mitigation plans, and FIAR oversight committee meeting minutes, which documented the results of DOD's efforts to prioritize and manage these risks. We interviewed the FIAR Director and other officials responsible for the FIAR Plan in the Office of the Under Secretary of Defense (Comptroller) and the Office of the Deputy Chief Management Officer (DCMO) to obtain an understanding of DOD's risk management process.

---

[5] GAO-11-851.

[6] We reviewed numerous risk management frameworks from industry, government, and academic sources. See GAO, "Appendix I: A Risk Management Framework" of *Risk Management: Further Refinements Needed to Assess Risks and Prioritize Protective Measures at Ports and Other Critical Infrastructure*, GAO-06-91 (Washington, D.C.: Dec. 15, 2005). Also, we determined that International Organization for Standardization 31000 *Risk Management – Principles and Guidelines* provides an internationally recognized framework with fundamental principles and guidelines for managing any form of risk in a systematic, transparent, and credible manner. We also used ch. 11 of the Project Management Institute's *The Standard for Program Management* and ch. 11 of *The Project Management Body of Knowledge*, which offers proven traditional practices for risk management as well as guidance for effective implementation of risk management.

[7] The NDAA for Fiscal Year 2010 mandated that DOD submit a report, not later than May 15 and November 15 of each year, to congressional defense committees on the status of the implementation of the FIAR Plan.

We also inquired about coordinated risk management efforts and about DOD's plans to revisit identified risks, identify new risks, and mitigate those risks.

Although the FIAR Directorate is responsible for DOD-wide risk management activities to implement the FIAR Plan, FIAR Directorate officials told us that some of DOD's component entities may have risk management activities under way. Accordingly, we made inquiries of the military components and two of the largest defense agencies—the Defense Finance and Accounting Service (DFAS) and the Defense Logistics Agency (DLA)—to identify those that had risk management efforts under way for implementing the FIAR Plan. Of these, the Department of the Navy (Navy) and DLA had risk management practices being implemented at the time of our review, and we included them for comparison purposes to the DOD-wide efforts. Using the five risk management guiding principles as criteria, we reviewed and analyzed the Navy's and DLA's risk management plans and supporting documents that identified, described, and prioritized risks to audit readiness as well as progress or status reports related to their efforts to address and monitor those risks. We also interviewed the Navy's and DLA's Financial Improvement Plan directors and other knowledgeable officials about their risk management processes and coordination with DOD's FIAR Director and the Office of the DCMO.

We conducted this performance audit from October 2011 to August 2013 in accordance with generally accepted government auditing standards. Those standards require that we plan and perform the audit to obtain sufficient, appropriate evidence to provide a reasonable basis for our findings and conclusions based on our audit objective. We believe that the evidence obtained provides a reasonable basis for our findings and conclusions based on our audit objective.

Background

In 2005, the DOD Comptroller established the FIAR Directorate, consisting of the FIAR Director and his staff, to develop, manage, and implement a strategic approach for addressing financial management deficiencies, achieving audit readiness, and integrating those efforts with other initiatives. Also in 2005, DOD first issued the FIAR Plan—a strategic plan and management tool for guiding, monitoring, and reporting on the department's ongoing financial management improvement efforts and for communicating the department's approach to addressing its financial management weaknesses and achieving financial statement audit readiness.

In August 2009, the DOD Comptroller sought to focus FIAR efforts by giving priority to improving processes and controls that support the financial information most often used to manage the department. Accordingly, the DOD Comptroller revised the FIAR Plan strategy to focus on two priorities—budgetary information and asset accountability. The first priority was to strengthen processes, controls, and systems that produce DOD's budgetary information. The second priority was to improve the accuracy and reliability of management information pertaining to the department's mission-critical assets, including military equipment, real property, and general equipment. In May 2010, the DOD Comptroller first issued the FIAR Guidance, which provided the standard methodology for the components—including the Departments of the Army, Navy, and Air Force and DLA—to implement the FIAR Plan. According to DOD, the components' successful implementation of this methodology is essential to the department's ability to achieve full financial statement auditability.

In recent years, legislation has reinforced certain DOD financial improvement goals and initiatives and has strengthened the role of DOD's Chief Management Officer (CMO).[8] For example, the NDAA for Fiscal Year 2010 tasked the CMO, in consultation with the DOD Comptroller, with the responsibility for developing and maintaining the FIAR Plan, and required the plan to describe the specific actions to be taken and the costs associated with validating audit readiness by the end of fiscal year 2017. This act also mandated that the department provide semiannual reports—no later than May 15 and November 15—on the status of its implementation of the FIAR Plan. In October 2011, the Secretary of Defense directed the department to achieve audit readiness for its SBR for general fund activities by the end of fiscal year 2014,[9] and the NDAA for Fiscal Year 2012 required that the next FIAR Plan update include a plan to support this goal. Most recently, the NDAA for Fiscal Year 2013 made the 2014 target for SBR auditability an ongoing component of the FIAR Plan by amending the NDAA for Fiscal Year 2010 such that it now explicitly refers to describing the actions and costs associated with validating as audit ready both DOD's SBR by the end of fiscal year 2014 and DOD's complete set of financial statements by the end of fiscal year 2017.

---

[8] By law, the Deputy Secretary of Defense is the CMO for DOD.

[9] An agency's general fund accounts are those accounts in the U.S. Treasury that hold all federal money not allocated by law to any other fund account.

Key Oversight Entities for the FIAR Effort

The department has established a FIAR governance hierarchy to oversee the FIAR Directorate's management and implementation of the FIAR Plan. At the top is the CMO, who approves the vision, goals, and priorities of the FIAR Plan, which are provided by the DOD Comptroller, in coordination with stakeholders within the department (e.g., military departments) as well as external stakeholders (e.g., the Office of Management and Budget and Congress). The CMO chairs the Deputy Management Action Group, which (1) provides advice and assistance to the CMO on matters pertaining to DOD enterprise management, business transformation, and operations and (2) reviews DOD component FIAR Plans and monitors their progress. To manage and oversee FIAR Plan implementation efforts, a number of committees and working groups, beginning with the FIAR Governance Board, have been established, as shown in table 1. The FIAR Governance Board engages the department's most senior leaders from the functional and financial communities and oversees DOD component progress. The FIAR Committee and Subcommittee oversee the management of the FIAR Plan. Descriptions of these key FIAR oversight bodies are presented below.

Table 1: Overview of DOD's Key FIAR Governance Entities

Governance entity	Description
FIAR Governance Board	• Co-chaired by the Comptroller and the DOD DCMO.
	• Members include military department DCMOs, military department assistant secretaries-financial management and comptroller, DOD functional community senior leaders (e.g., the Assistant Secretary-Logistics and Material Readiness), and DOD Office of Inspector General (OIG) (advisory member).
	• Meets quarterly to provide leadership and oversight of the department's FIAR Plan and to identify risks that could prevent the department from achieving its goals.
FIAR Committee	• Chaired by the Deputy Chief Financial Officer.
	• Members include FIAR Director; military department deputy assistant secretaries for financial operations; Director for Audit Readiness, DFAS; Director, Accounting and Finance Policy and Analysis, Office of the Under Secretary of Defense (Comptroller); and Assistant Inspector General, DFAS, DOD OIG (advisory members).
	• Meets monthly or more often if needed.
	• Provides advice and recommendations to the FIAR Governance Board on ways to prioritize, integrate, and manage efforts to improve financial management and achieve audit readiness.

Governance entity	Description
FIAR Subcommittee	• Chaired by FIAR Director.
	• Members include financial operations representatives from each military component, DLA, and DFAS as well as the Assistant Inspector General, DFAS, OIG (advisory member).
	• Meets monthly or more often if needed.
	• Provides support and advice to the FIAR Committee on ways to further improve financial management and assists in developing detailed guidance and solutions to issues.

Sources: November 2012 FIAR Plan Status Report, Committee Charters, and GAO-11-851.

DOD's Reported Status of the FIAR Effort and Projected Budget for Audit Readiness

In the November 2012 FIAR Plan Status Report, DOD reported the following:

- Fifteen percent of the department's reported general fund budgetary resources were undergoing audits, including the Marine Corps' budgetary resources. The military departments, defense agencies, and other components were preparing the remaining budgetary resources to be ready for audit by the end of September 2014.

- For mission-critical assets, DOD reported that 4 percent of these assets were undergoing audits, 37 percent had been validated as audit ready, 12 percent had been asserted as audit ready by the respective component,[10] and the remaining 47 percent were being prepared for audit readiness assertions.

DOD's projected funding for the FIAR effort for fiscal years 2012 through 2018 is shown in table 2.

---

[10] Components are supposed to assert audit readiness to the FIAR Directorate after they have taken sufficient actions to correct internal control weaknesses and have sufficient documentation to support information such as the authorization, approval, validity, and completeness of financial transactions.

Table 2: DOD's Reported Audit Readiness Resources

Dollars in millions

	Fiscal year						
	2012	2013	2014	2015	2016	2017	2018
Audit readiness							
Process review and remediation	$232	$422	$416	$288	$218	$182	$181
DFAS audit readiness support	40	58	52	43	43	43	43
Internal audit cost	18	18	24	23	23	23	23
Audit readiness subtotal	$290	$498	$492	$354	$284	$248	$247
Validation and audits	18	44	71	127	117	127	127
Financial systems	95	116	93	78	80	68	32
Total audit readiness resources	**$403**	**$658**	**$656**	**$559**	**$481**	**$443**	**$406**

Source: DOD FIAR Plan Status Report, November 2012.

Risk Management

Risk management is a strategy for helping program managers and stakeholders make decisions about assessing risk, allocating resources, and taking actions under conditions of uncertainty. Risk management can be applied to an entire organization, at its many levels, or to specific functions, projects, and activities. While risk management does not provide absolute assurance regarding the achievement of an organization's objectives, an effective risk management strategy can be particularly useful in a decentralized organization—such as DOD—to help top management identify potential problems and reasonably allocate resources to address them. Leading risk management practices recommend that organizations develop, implement, and continuously improve a process for managing risk and integrate it into the organization's overall governance, strategy, policies, planning, management, and reporting processes. When planning for risk, an organization determines the methodology, strategies, scope, and parameters for managing risks to the objective.

In researching risk management principles, we identified five basic guiding principles of risk management, as shown in figure 1.

Figure 1: Five Basic Guiding Principles of Risk Management

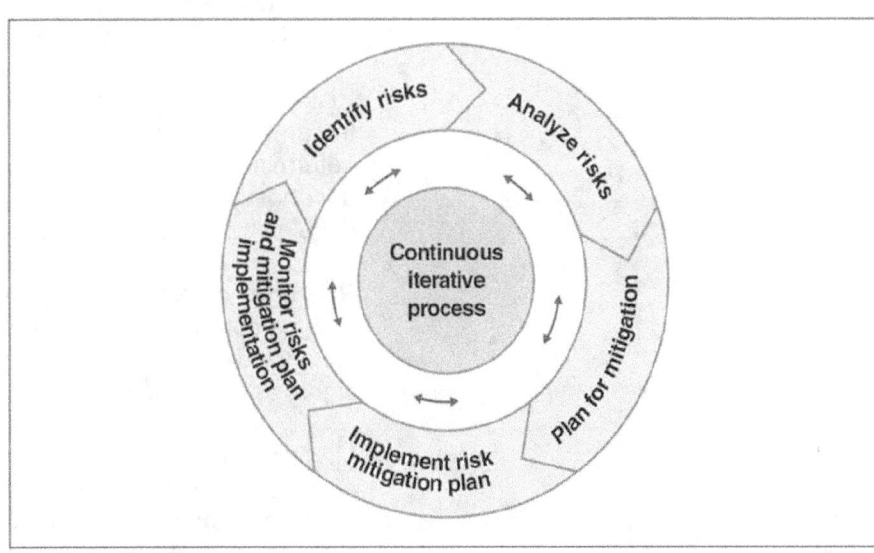

Source: GAO.

- **Identify risks.** The goal of risk identification is to generate a comprehensive list of risks, regardless of whether those risks are under the control of the organization, based on events that could significantly affect the achievement of objectives. Risk identification involves continuous and iterative communication and consultation with internal and external stakeholders to identify new risks, sources of risk, areas these risks affect, events (including changes in circumstances), their causes (root causes), and potential consequences to the objective. This can be performed through additional inquiry with subject matter experts, surveying and interviewing experienced executives, high-level and detailed documentation reviews, checklists based on historical information, and diagramming processes.

- **Analyze risks.** Risk analysis involves developing an understanding of identified risks to assist management in determining the most appropriate methods and strategies in prioritizing and responding to risk. It requires risks to be analyzed to determine the impact of interdependencies between the overall program risks and program component risks. According to guiding principles, risk analysis is a vital part of the entire risk management process as it helps managers determine where to focus their attention and allocate resources to maximize the likelihood of achieving objectives. This requires management to consult with key stakeholders, project managers, and experts to discuss, analyze, and rank risks based on their expert analysis. Suggested techniques for risk analysis include the following:

○ Risk categorization. Risks can be categorized by sources of risk, the area of the program affected, or other useful categories to determine the areas of the program most exposed to the effects of uncertainty. Grouping risks by common root causes can lead to developing effective risk responses.

○ Risk urgency assessment. Risks requiring near-term responses may be considered more urgent to address. Indicators of priority can include time to affect a risk response, symptoms and warning signs, and the risk rating.

○ Modeling. This includes techniques that can be used to assess the effect of risk interdependencies (i.e., one risk is dependent on another risk being resolved) with specific attention to life cycle program costs.[11] Examples include (1) sensitivity analysis, which helps to determine which risks have the most potential impact on the program, and (2) financial analysis methods, such as life cycle program costs, return on investment, or cost benefit analysis, which helps to determine the viability, stability, and profitability of a program.

• **Plan for risk mitigation.** Planning for risk mitigation entails selecting the most appropriate and timely action to address risks while balancing the costs and efforts of implementation against the benefits derived. The mitigating actions must also be realistic, achievable, measurable, and documented. Among other things, the plan should include the point of contact responsible for addressing each risk, the root causes of the risk, the options for mitigation, risk status, contingency actions or fallback approach, and resource needs.

• **Implement risk mitigation plan.** Implementing the risk mitigation plan determines what planning, budget, requirements, contractual changes, or a combination of these is needed; provides a coordination vehicle for management and other stakeholders; directs the team to execute the defined and approved risk mitigation plans; outlines the

---

[11] Life cycle costs are the total costs to develop, plan, implement, and monitor a program.

risk reporting requirements for ongoing monitoring; and documents the history of changes.

- **Monitor risks and mitigation plan implementation.** Effective tracking of risk mitigation implementation (risk monitoring) provides information that assists managers with making effective decisions before problems occur by continually monitoring mitigation plans for new and changing risks. Risk monitoring is the process of identifying, analyzing, and planning for new risks; tracking identified risks; and reanalyzing existing risks throughout the life of the program. Monitoring is also intended to help management determine whether program assumptions are still valid and whether proper risk management policies and procedures are being followed.

Risk management is an iterative process and these guiding principles are interdependent such that deficiencies in implementing one guiding principle will cause deficiencies in performing other guiding principles. For example, if the procedures for identifying risks are not comprehensive and not all significant risks are identified, then the other guiding principles for risk management will not be carried out for any risks not identified. Similarly, if identified risks are not sufficiently analyzed, then it is less likely that effective risk mitigation plans will be developed.

DOD Has Not Established an Effective Risk Management Process

DOD carried out some risk management practices centrally with respect to implementing the FIAR Plan, but did not follow many risk management principles necessary for effective risk management and did not document its risk management policies and procedures. Specifically, DOD identified some risks to its FIAR effort, but its risk identification procedures were not comprehensive or documented. In addition, its procedures for analyzing, mitigating, and monitoring risks were also undocumented and did not adhere to guiding principles. We found, however, that two DOD components—the Navy and DLA—had documented risk management processes that were consistent with many of the guiding principles for effective risk management.

Identification of Risks to FIAR Implementation Was Incomplete

Source: GAO.

Although DOD has identified several risks that could hinder its efforts to achieve financial statement auditability, it did not identify or address additional key risks that were reported in external audit reports. In January 2012, DOD identified six risks that if not mitigated, could impede its efforts to achieve auditability.[12] The department included these risks in its May 2012 semiannual FIAR Plan Status report. The following is DOD's summary of the six risks it identified.

1. A lack of DOD-wide commitment. Stakeholders must be committed to improving controls and providing supporting documentation.

2. Insufficient accountability. Leaders and managers must be incentivized to achieve FIAR goals.

3. Poorly defined scope and requirements. Financial improvement plans should address accounting requirements important to audit success.

4. Unqualified or inexperienced personnel. DOD must ensure that personnel are capable of making and supporting judgments that auditors will agree meet accounting standards.

5. Insufficient funding. Resources must be aligned to the scope and scale of the FIAR effort.

6. Information system control weaknesses. Many processes and controls reside entirely in software applications, and therefore these systems and interfaces must support complete and accurate records.

DOD did not have written policies and procedures or a documented process for identifying these risks; however, DOD officials told us that they held internal management meetings, brainstormed with internal and external stakeholders, and reviewed prior GAO and DOD Inspector General (IG) reports. While DOD's identification of risks was a positive step, DOD did not identify sufficient information about these risks, such as the source, root cause, the audit area(s) the risk will impact, and potential consequences to the program if the risk is not effectively mitigated—all

---

[12] DOD initially documented these risks for risk management purposes in briefing slides for the January 2012 FIAR Governance Board meeting.

critical to properly analyze and prioritize risk. Further, DOD's risk identification process did not identify all significant risks to achieving its auditability goals.

DOD officials told us that risk management practices were embedded throughout the FIAR process and that these six risks were identified in whole or in part through this process. Specifically, they said that monthly and quarterly meetings of the various FIAR oversight committees included ongoing discussions with DOD components regarding their progress in meeting FIAR goals and milestones. According to guiding principles, agencies should generate a comprehensive list of risks based on those events that might create, enhance, prevent, degrade, accelerate, or delay the achievement of objectives. In addition, guiding principles state that risk identification is an iterative process where program stakeholders continually forecast the outcomes of current strategies, plans, and activities and exercise their best judgment to identify new risks as the program progresses throughout its life cycle. Although DOD indicated that risks are discussed on an ongoing basis during various meetings, the risks it initially identified were not comprehensive, and it did not provide evidence of efforts to identify additional risks.

We identified additional risks based on prior audit work. For example, DOD did not identify risks related to (1) the components' reliance on service providers for significant aspects of their financial operations, such as processing and recording financial transactions, and (2) the lack of a department-wide effort to follow documentation retention standards to ensure that required audit support can be provided to auditors. We did not attempt to identify all significant risks to DOD's audit readiness effort, but these two examples indicate that DOD did not identify all significant risks to the FIAR effort. Conducting a risk identification process in accordance with guiding principles would have increased the likelihood of DOD identifying additional risks that could impede the department's ability to achieve its auditability goals. As noted previously, the guiding principles are interdependent, and deficiencies in the identification of risks will hinder implementation of other guiding principles, such as risk mitigation.

Reliance on service providers: The Marine Corps received a disclaimer of opinion on its fiscal years 2010 and 2011 SBRs because of its inability to provide timely and complete responses to audit documentation requests. Specifically, the DOD IG reported that DFAS—the service provider responsible for performing accounting, disbursing, and financial reporting services for the Marine Corps—did not have effective procedures in place to ensure that supporting documentation for transactions was complete and readily available to support basic audit transaction testing.[13] In December 2011,[14] we reported that the Navy and Marine Corps could not reconcile their Fund Balance with Treasury accounts in large part because they depend on DFAS to maintain the data necessary for the reconciliation,[15] and DFAS did not maintain reliable data or the documentation necessary to complete the reconciliation.

DOD officials stated that although they did not identify the reliance on service providers as a risk, they recognized it as a challenge and, as a result, developed requirements in the FIAR Guidance. The FIAR Guidance requires the service providers to have their control activities and supporting documentation examined by the DOD IG or an independent auditor in accordance with Statement on Standards for Attestation Engagements (SSAE) 16 so that reporting entities (components) have a basis for relying on the service provider's data for their financial statement audits.[16] To prepare for an SSAE 16 examination, the FIAR Guidance requires a service provider first to evaluate its control activities and supporting documentation, take corrective actions as necessary, and then assert audit readiness to the FIAR Directorate. Once the FIAR Directorate validates that the service provider has sufficient controls and supporting documentation, the service provider can then engage an auditor to conduct an SSAE 16 audit examination.

The FIAR Guidance states that service providers should identify the reporting components' audit readiness assertion dates so that they can complete SSAE 16 examinations in time to meet the components' needs. However, the November 2012 FIAR Plan Status Report indicates that key service providers will not have SSAE 16 examinations completed until

---

[13] GAO-11-830.

[14] GAO, *DOD Financial Management: Ongoing Challenges with Reconciling Navy and Marine Corps Fund Balance with Treasury*, GAO-12-132 (Washington, D.C.: Dec. 20, 2011).

[15] Fund Balance with Treasury is an asset account that reflects the available budget spending authority of federal agencies. Collections and disbursements by agencies will, correspondingly, increase or decrease the balance in the account.

[16] SSAE 16 provides standards for auditors to follow for reporting on controls at organizations that provide services to user entities when those controls are likely to be relevant to user entities' internal control over financial reporting.

sometime in fiscal year 2014. DOD components need to rely on the results of SSAE 16 examinations of key service providers so that the components can effectively assess their own controls in accordance with the FIAR Guidance. In light of the expected completion dates of SSAE 16 examinations, it is not clear if components will have sufficient time to carry out the activities necessary to test and validate their own controls and assert audit readiness for their SBRs by September 2014.

For these reasons, the requirements in the FIAR Guidance have not fully mitigated the risk associated with the reliance on DOD's service providers. Although DOD recognized this issue as a challenge, the reliance on service providers was not identified by DOD management as a significant risk to DOD achieving audit readiness. If DOD formally identified the reliance on service providers as a risk, it is more likely to manage and monitor this risk in accordance with risk management guiding principles.

Need for supporting documentation: Document retention and the ability to provide supporting documentation for transactions have been pervasive problems throughout DOD. For example, during the Marine Corps audits, the DOD IG found that DFAS had only retained selected pages of the documents supporting payment vouchers, such as the voucher cover sheet, and did not have critical items, such as the purchase order, receiving report, and invoice, to support that payments were made as required.[17] In addition, we reported in March 2012 that the Army did not have an efficient or effective process or system for providing supporting documentation for its military payroll expenses and, as a result, was unable to locate or provide supporting personnel documents for our statistical sample of fiscal year 2010 Army military pay accounts.[18]

DOD officials told us that they recognized document retention as a challenge, and that this issue was addressed in the FIAR Guidance as well as in DOD's Financial Management Regulation (FMR) and

---

[17] Department of Defense, Office of Inspector General, *Independent Auditors Report on the Marine Corps General Fund FY2010 and FY2009 Combined Statement of Budgetary Resources*, DODIG-2011-009 (Washington, D.C.: Nov. 8, 2010), and *Independent Auditors Report on the Marine Corps General Fund FY2011 and FY2010 Combined Statement of Budgetary Resources*, DODIG-2012-016 (Washington, D.C.: Nov. 7, 2011).

[18] GAO, *DOD Financial Management: The Army Faces Significant Challenges in Achieving Audit Readiness for Its Military Pay*, GAO-12-406 (Washington, D.C.: Mar. 22, 2012).

requirements established by the National Archives and Records Administration (NARA).[19] Both the FIAR Guidance and the FMR refer to NARA for guidance on record retention, and the FIAR Guidance also refers to Standards for Internal Control in the Federal Government.[20] However, neither the FIAR Guidance nor the FMR was specific enough to ensure that the documents needed to support audit readiness were retained and available in a timely manner. For example, the FIAR Guidance and the FMR did not address which types of documentation to retain and the required time frames for retaining these documents, thus leaving these decisions to the judgment of DOD component personnel responsible for preparing for audit readiness. DOD officials informed us that they were in the process of updating the FMR to address documentation types and retention periods; however, the updated guidance was not yet available at the time of our review. As a result, we could not determine how and to what extent a revised FMR would address document retention issues.

Continuous and comprehensive risk identification is critical because, if a risk is not formally identified, it is less likely to be managed effectively and in accordance with risk management guiding principles. The first step to managing and mitigating risks is to identify them. For example, if DOD had identified the reliance on service providers and the need for document retention standards as risks, it might have implemented actions to address these risks sooner so that they would not have been major impediments to Navy, Marine Corps, and Army audit readiness efforts. If risks to the FIAR effort are not comprehensively identified, DOD is less likely to take the actions necessary to mitigate or minimize the risks and therefore less likely to meet its audit readiness goals.

Navy's and DLA's Risk Identification

Both the Navy and DLA employed techniques that are consistent with guiding principles for risk identification. For example, they collaborated with stakeholders, experts, support personnel, and project managers on a weekly or monthly basis to discuss potential new risks to the audit effort using techniques such as brainstorming, interviewing key stakeholders, diagramming, and SWOT (strengths, weaknesses, opportunities, and

---

[19] The DOD FMR directs statutory and regulatory financial management requirements, systems, and functions for all appropriated and non-appropriated, working capital, revolving, and trust fund activities within DOD.

[20] GAO, *Standards for Internal Control in the Federal Government*, GAO/AIMD-00-21.3.1 (Washington, D.C.: November 1999).

threats) analysis, and documented the results in risk registers or risk databases. Both the Navy's and DLA's identified risks included the reliance on service providers and the need for better document retention.

Risk Analysis of FIAR Implementation Was Incomplete

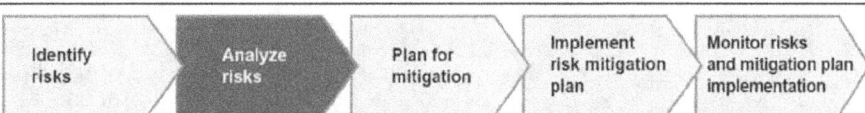

Source: GAO.

DOD did not follow guiding principles for performing risk analysis. The FIAR Director plotted the six risks DOD identified on graphs that were intended to show the likelihood of the risks occurring (or probability) and the effect (or impact) on the overall implementation of the FIAR Plan (see fig. 2).

Figure 2: DOD's Probability and Impact Matrix for Risk Analysis

❶ Lack of DoD-wide Commitment and Action

❷ Insufficient Accountability

❸ Poor Scope and Requirements

❹ Unqualified or Inexperienced Personnel

❺ Insufficient Funding

❻ IT System Control Weaknesses

Source: Quarterly FIAR Governance Board Meeting briefing slides, January 2012.

The FIAR Director said that he did not consult with key stakeholders, project managers, and experts to analyze these risks as suggested by guiding principles. He also stated that he did not use recommended analytical techniques, such as (1) risk categorization, (2) risk urgency assessment, or (3) sensitivity analysis. In addition, the FIAR Director did not perform an assessment to determine the individual DOD components' ability to achieve audit readiness. For example, if one DOD component has significantly more information technology system control weaknesses or fewer skilled personnel than another DOD component, it is likely to have a higher risk of not achieving audit readiness. Performing effective risk analysis could enable DOD to develop appropriate risk mitigation plans to address such concerns, including resource allocation among the components.

A probability and impact matrix is generally used for both communication and prioritization. Guiding principles state that risk analysis is a vital part of the risk management process because it helps management determine the most appropriate methods and strategies for mitigating risks. In addition, it allows management to better allocate resources to maximize the likelihood of achieving objectives. By not analyzing risks in accordance with guiding principles, DOD increased the likelihood that it would not adequately address the most critical risks in a timely manner.

Navy's and DLA's Risk Analysis

Navy and DLA officials generally followed guiding principles for risk analysis. For example, at both the Navy and DLA, project management teams worked together to determine who was primarily responsible for managing each identified risk. The Navy and DLA employed analytical techniques to assess risk and documented the results of their analyses—such as the impact each risk has or could have on the objectives and the risk's priority—in risk registers. In addition, both the Navy and DLA documented their risk analysis processes to allow for consistent implementation. As a result of these analyses, Navy identified the following as its three highest risks to audit readiness efforts: (1) reliance on service providers, (2) internal resources in information technology operations, and (3) tracking unmatched disbursements, while DLA identified (1) data access limitations, (2) standard accounting and financial management functions, and (3) audit response capabilities as its three highest risks. The Navy and DLA each considered its respective risks to have a high impact on audit readiness and a high probability of occurrence.

Planning for Risk Mitigation Actions Was Not Detailed or Sufficient

Source: GAO.

The DOD FIAR Directorate developed risk mitigation plans first published in the May 2012 FIAR Plan Status Report. However, DOD did not have documented policies and detailed procedures for planning risk mitigation actions. As a result, its plans did not have most of the elements recommended by guiding principles. For example, the plans did not include (1) assignment of responsibility or ownership of the risk mitigation actions, (2) information about DOD's or the components' roles and responsibilities in executing these plans, (3) deadlines or milestones for individual mitigation actions, and (4) resource needs.

The lack of details makes it difficult to determine whether the planned risk mitigation actions are sufficient to address the risks. For example, the risk mitigation plan for addressing the risk of unqualified or inexperienced personnel did not provide sufficient information as recommended by guiding principles. According to the plan, DOD intends to

- hire experienced individuals who are certified public accountants (CPA),

- hire independent public accounting firms to help the department prepare for audit,

- provide FIAR training to the appropriate functional and financial employees,

- modify existing military department training and education programs to include FIAR objectives, and

- conduct limited-scope audits of portions of the financial statements to provide firsthand experience in preparation for future financial statement audits.

However, the mitigation plan did not provide further details, such as the following:

- DOD's actions to comply with the mandate, included in the NDAA for Fiscal Year 2010,[21] to prepare a strategic workforce plan and conduct a gap analysis for mission-critical skills in its civilian workforce,[22] including those in its financial management community. As we

---

[21] The NDAA for Fiscal Year 2010, Pub. L. No. 111-84, § 1108(a), 123 Stat. 2190, 2488 (Oct. 28, 2009), *codified as amended at* 10 U.S.C. § 115b, enacted a recurring strategic workforce plan requirement similar to one originally included in the NDAA for Fiscal Year 2006, Pub. L. No. 109-163, 119 Stat. 3136, 3452 (Jan. 6, 2006) which was set to expire after 2010R-127.

[22] A gap analysis identifies deficiencies in current workforce skill sets and projects workforce requirements for the future.

recently reported,[23] DOD has not completed any of its competency gap analyses for financial management.

- How many CPAs DOD plans to hire, in what capacity these CPAs will be utilized, what components will be involved, and at what cost.

- The relevant criteria for determining which employees should attend new FIAR training, whether training is mandatory, and how many employees are affected.

- How DOD's financial management certification program would coincide with the current mandatory training.

- How or which existing training and education programs would be modified, the time frames for doing so, the intent of the modifications (i.e., how this training would differ from FIAR training), and which employees will be attending these classes.

DOD FIAR officials stated that their mitigation plans were straightforward and did not require additional detail for implementation purposes. However, as discussed earlier, guiding principles state that effective planning ensures that the activities to be performed to achieve the objectives are realistic, known, and understood by those who are responsible for performing them, including the milestones and available resources. Without sufficiently detailed plans for risk mitigation, achieving the program's overall objectives—financial management improvements and auditability—is at increased risk of failure.

Navy's and DLA's Risk Mitigation Plans

The Navy and DLA included risk mitigation plans for each of their identified risks in their risk registers. The plans documented the mitigation strategy, assignment of responsibility or ownership of the risk mitigation actions, status updates, and the potential impact of the risk on the objectives.

---

[23] GAO, *Human Capital: DOD Needs Complete Assessments to Improve Future Civilian Strategic Workforce Plans*, GAO-12-1014 (Washington, D.C.: Sept. 27, 2012).

Information on Implementation of Risk Mitigation Actions Was Limited

Source: GAO.

The DOD FIAR Directorate did not maintain documentation of specific mitigation actions taken or who performed them. Specifically, evidence of risk mitigation actions provided by the FIAR Directorate consisted of metrics reported each month and each quarter to the key oversight entities, such as the FIAR Governance Board and FIAR Committee. According to FIAR Directorate officials, they compiled these metrics—related to such matters as the total attendance at FIAR training classes and the number of information technology systems assessed—based largely on information self-reported by the components. The FIAR Directorate did not independently validate this information for reliability as suggested by guiding principles.

We found that the reported metrics did not provide a complete picture of the status of the department's efforts to implement its risk mitigation action plan. Specifically, the metrics did not provide the details needed to determine what actions had been taken, their status and impact, who performed the work, the resources used, the remaining resource needs, and the actions still to be taken. The FIAR Director did not provide an explanation for how these particular metrics were selected for reporting or why more information about mitigation actions was not reported. DOD did not have policies and procedures requiring DOD to (1) document the implementation of mitigation actions, (2) develop appropriate metrics, and (3) validate reported metrics. If DOD does not effectively measure its progress in the implementation of risk mitigation plans, it cannot sufficiently manage risk mitigation actions and monitor the extent to which they are or are not succeeding. Without such information, DOD is limited in its ability to make informed decisions about ongoing mitigation efforts, adjust course as necessary, and identify and mitigate any new risks. This, in turn, could adversely affect DOD's ability to meet the mandated deadlines of an audit-ready SBR by fiscal year 2014 and audit-ready consolidated financial statements by fiscal year 2017.

The following are examples of two of DOD's identified risks wherein the reported risk management metrics did not adequately measure DOD's progress in implementing its risk mitigation plans.

- **Unqualified or inexperienced personnel.** To address this risk, the November 2012 FIAR Plan Status Report stated that DOD is hiring experienced individuals who are CPAs, modifying existing training programs, and providing FIAR training to employees. DOD reported one metric for this risk, which relates to attendance at FIAR training classes. However, DOD's metrics did not address the number of CPAs hired or to be hired, who is responsible for the hiring, or the progress to date in hiring experienced personnel. Moreover, the reported metric related to FIAR training classes did not provide key information for assessing progress. As of January 2013, DOD components reported that approximately 7,000 of their financial management personnel had attended FIAR training classes. However, DOD acknowledged that this metric likely included some individuals who were counted multiple times. For example, an individual who attended each of the six FIAR training courses would be counted six times. As a result, it was unclear how many staff members had taken the training courses. In addition, the metrics did not identify the total number of DOD's approximately 58,000 financial management personnel who are required or expected to take these training courses. As a result, DOD's "Total Attendance at FIAR Training" metric did not provide a meaningful measure of progress against the identified risk of unqualified and inexperienced personnel.

- **Information system control weaknesses**. DOD engaged the DCMO to oversee development and implementation for enterprise resource planning (ERP) business system modernization and has required ERP deployment plans to be integrated with components' financial improvement plans to mitigate risks of information system control weaknesses.[24] However, DOD's metric for information systems control weaknesses focuses on the number of information technology systems that have been assessed against the Federal Information System Controls Audit Manual (FISCAM) requirements.[25] As of January 2013, DOD components reported that only 18 of 140 information technology systems had been assessed against FISCAM requirements. This metric does not provide needed details, such as the number of systems assessed that were found to be noncompliant with FISCAM requirements, the number of system change requests

---

[24] An ERP system is an automated system using commercial off-the-shelf software consisting of multiple, integrated functional modules that perform a variety of business-related tasks, such as general ledger accounting, payroll, and supply chain management.

[25] FISCAM is a methodology for performing information system control audits of federal and other governmental entities in accordance with professional standards.

identified or completed, and the status of corrective actions.[26] Moreover, the 140 systems identified in DOD's metric may not constitute the total universe of relevant financial management systems; as we recently reported, DOD had identified 310 financial management systems.[27]

In addition, DOD's identified risk regarding information system internal control weaknesses represented a very broad area of risk. The metrics did not address a number of more specific risks identified by DOD IG audits, such as risks related to implementation of ERP systems, including schedule slippages and cost overruns related to those systems, and the increasing possibility of having to rely on legacy systems to achieve audit readiness. For example, the FIAR Directorate reported that ERP systems are necessary for DOD to produce auditable financial statements.[28] However, the DOD IG found that six ERP systems experienced cost overruns of $8 billion and schedule delays ranging from 1.5 to 12.5 years during system development and implementation.[29] As a result of the schedule delays, the DOD IG reported that DOD will continue using outdated legacy systems and diminish the estimated savings from business system modernization, further putting at risk DOD's ability to achieve its audit readiness goals. We had previously reported similar issues in our March 2012 report.[30] The DOD IG also found that the DCMO and other DOD officials were relying on components' program management offices' self-compliance assertions when they certified and approved funding of over $300 million for the six ERP systems, and did not review the business processes or verify the reliability of the components' program management office's submissions as required by the NDAA for Fiscal Year 2010. As a result, DOD faces increased risks of

---

[26] A system change request is a request to change or adjust components in an information technology system.

[27] GAO, *DOD Business Systems Modernization: Governance Mechanisms for Implementing Management Controls Need to Be Improved*, GAO-12-685 (Washington, D.C.: June 1, 2012).

[28] GAO, *DOD Financial Management: Reported Status of Department of Defense's Enterprise Resource Planning Systems*, GAO-12-565R (Washington, D.C.: Mar. 30, 2012).

[29] Department of Defense, Office of Inspector General, *Enterprise Resource Planning Systems Schedule Delays and Reengineering Weaknesses Increase Risks to DOD's Auditability Goals*, DODIG-2012-111 (Washington, D.C.: September 2012).

[30] GAO-12-565R.

ERP systems incurring additional cost increases and schedule delays that could affect its ability to achieve an auditable SBR by 2014 and a complete set of auditable financial statements by 2017. As noted previously, if DOD had been more specific in its identification of risks related to its information systems, it would have been in a better position to analyze these risks and develop effective mitigation plans to address them.

Navy's and DLA's Risk Mitigation Plan Implementation

Navy and DLA officials document their risk implementation efforts by including status updates on a weekly or monthly basis for each risk in their risk registers. The Navy's risk register had detailed status updates for each risk that included the current status of mitigation efforts and any updates or additional comments that need to be addressed. DLA's risk register indicated whether risk mitigation efforts were under way (active) for each risk. DLA also identified events (triggers) for each risk that provided an alert as to when a certain risk was close to being realized or imminent, which could then initiate the next course of action.

Monitoring of Mitigation Actions to Address FIAR Implementation Risk Was Not Sufficient

Source: GAO.

DOD officials, including those in the FIAR Directorate and key FIAR oversight entities such as the FIAR Governance Board and the FIAR Committee, were monitoring risk mitigation efforts using the metrics previously discussed. However, these metrics do not provide the information that managers need to (1) track identified risks and assess the effectiveness of implemented mitigation actions, (2) make effective decisions, and (3) identify and plan for new risks. Further, our review of oversight committee meeting minutes did not find evidence that the metrics were discussed in any greater detail or that decisions were made based on these metrics.

If DOD is not effectively monitoring risks, it may be unaware of deficiencies in risk mitigation action plans or implementation that may weaken the effectiveness of its risk mitigation. Guiding principles state that risk monitoring reduces the impact of risk by identifying, analyzing, reporting, and managing risks on a continuous basis for the life of the program. Moreover, if DOD management does not follow guiding principles for monitoring risks to the FIAR effort, it lacks assurance that the department is doing all it can to ensure the success of its audit readiness efforts. Also at risk are the substantial resources that DOD estimates it will need to become audit ready. Based on the data in table 2, DOD's reported audit readiness resources will average approximately $515 million annually over 7 years. Without the awareness gained through effective monitoring, DOD will not have the information it needs to proactively respond to new risks or adjust its plans based on lessons learned in a manner that can benefit the entire department. For example, as we have previously reported, the Marine Corps' unsuccessful attempts to have its SBR audited for fiscal years 2010 and 2011 have resulted in lessons learned that may be helpful to other components in preparing for audit readiness.[31]

Navy's and DLA's Risk Monitoring

Navy and DLA officials told us that they monitor their risk management efforts during their weekly and monthly meetings that include risk owners and their internal financial management oversight teams. Those meetings are used to discuss new risks, update risk registers, and provide status updates and feedback to component managers about the status of audit readiness efforts.

Conclusions

In light of current budget constraints and fiscal pressures throughout the federal government and particularly at DOD, it is more important than ever for DOD to have reliable information with which to manage its resources effectively and efficiently. This necessity and DOD's estimated costs for the FIAR effort make the successful implementation of its FIAR Plan even more imperative. DOD has taken some actions to manage its department-level risks associated with preparing auditable financial statements through its FIAR Plan. However, DOD had not followed most risk management guiding principles, and had not designed and implemented written policies and procedures to fully identify and manage risks affecting implementation of the FIAR Plan. DOD identified some risks to the FIAR effort, but its risk identification process was not comprehensive. Moreover, DOD did not sufficiently analyze the risks, plan and implement mitigation actions, and monitor the results.

To improve management of the risks to the FIAR effort throughout the department, the risk management processes established by two DOD components—the Navy and DLA—could serve as a starting point.

---

[31] GAO, *DOD Financial Management: Marine Corps Statement of Budgetary Resources Audit Results and Lessons Learned*, GAO-11-830 (Washington, D.C.: Sept. 15, 2011).

Ineffective management of the risks to successful implementation of the FIAR Plan increases the likelihood that DOD will not achieve its audit readiness goals.

Recommendations for Executive Action

We recommend that the Secretary of Defense direct the Under Secretary of Defense, in his capacity as the Chief Management Officer and in consultation with the Under Secretary of Defense (Comptroller), to take the following two actions:

- Design and implement department-level policies and detailed procedures for FIAR Plan risk management that incorporate the five guiding principles for effective risk management. The following are examples of key features of each of the guiding principles that DOD should, at a minimum, address in its policies and procedures.

  o Identify risks. Generate a comprehensive and continuously updated list of risks that includes the root cause of each risk, audit area(s) each risk will affect, and the potential consequences if a risk is not effectively mitigated.

  o Analyze risks. Consult with key stakeholders, including program managers; use analytical techniques, such as risk categorization, risk urgency assessment, or sensitivity analysis; and determine the impact of the identified risks on individual DOD components' abilities to achieve audit readiness.

  o Plan for risk mitigation. Assign responsibility or ownership of the risk mitigation actions, define roles and responsibilities in executing mitigation plans, establish deadlines or milestones for individual mitigation actions, and estimate resource needs.

  o Implement risk mitigation plan. Document the implementation of mitigation actions, develop appropriate metrics that allow for tracking of progress, and validate reported metrics.

  o Monitor risks. Track identified risks and assess the effectiveness of implemented mitigation actions on a continuous basis, including identifying and planning for new risks.

- Consider and incorporate, as appropriate, the Navy's and DLA's risk management practices in department-level policies and procedures.

Agency Comments and Our Evaluation

DOD officials provided written comments on a draft of this report, which are reprinted in appendix I. DOD acknowledged that it does not have a written risk management policy specifically related to the FIAR effort, but did not concur with our assessment of the department's overall risk management of the FIAR initiative. However, DOD cited planned actions that are consistent with our recommendations and findings, including (1) improving the documentation related to FIAR risk management activities, (2) reinforcing the importance of more detailed risk management activity within each DOD component executing its detailed FIAR Plan, (3) reinstating the DOD probability and impact matrix for risk analysis for the FIAR initiative, and (4) reevaluating all metrics used to monitor progress and risk for audit readiness and developing new measures as appropriate. DOD's planned actions, if implemented effectively and efficiently, would help address some aspects of the five guiding principles of risk management that are the basis for our recommendations. While these are good first steps, we continue to believe additional action is warranted. Consequently, we reaffirm our recommendations.

DOD stated that its risk management processes and activities were embedded into the design of the FIAR initiative. DOD also stated that all common risk management activities were occurring, including identification, evaluation, remediation, and monitoring of enterprise-wide risks for the FIAR initiative, and these activities were effectively managing risk. As stated in our report, while DOD does have some aspects of risk management activities under way in each of these areas, these activities do not go far enough in addressing most risk management guiding principles, nor has DOD designed and implemented written policies and procedures to fully identify and manage risks affecting implementation of the FIAR Plan. For example, although DOD identified six enterprise-wide risks through its risk identification process, DOD did not provide any evidence that the six identified risks were reevaluated on a continuous basis or that new risks were identified or discussed. Additionally, DOD did not identify sufficient details about these risks, such as the root cause, areas the risks will affect, and consequences to the program if a risk is not effectively mitigated nor did it develop a comprehensive list of risks.

As noted in our report, we identified at least two additional risks that could impede DOD's ability to achieve audit readiness—reliance on service providers and lack of documentation standards. DOD's response noted that it did not label these as risks but as challenges and had actions under way to address them. While we commend DOD for taking some actions to address these two issues, by not adding them to the formal list of risks during the risk identification process, they may not undergo the same level of risk analysis, mitigation, and monitoring as the six formally identified risks.

In addition, DOD did not agree with our finding that its planned mitigation actions lacked details and made it difficult to determine whether the planned actions were sufficient to address the risk. For example, we reported that DOD's mitigation plans did not address specific details related to its mitigating actions for the risk of unqualified or inexperienced personnel, such as the number of CPAs or experienced personnel the department planned to hire, relevant criteria to determine which personnel would attend FIAR training, timing of the DOD financial management certification program, and how existing training and education programs will be modified. In response to our report, DOD provided additional details related to its mitigating actions to address this risk, which were not previously provided to us or reported in the FIAR Plan status updates, including time frames for implementing some of its mitigating actions. However, DOD's additional details still do not address the findings in our report or issues related to the timing for implementing planned mitigation actions, as many actions are to be implemented beginning in fiscal years 2013 and 2014. This raises concerns about whether DOD can effectively manage and mitigate risks in time to meet its audit readiness goals, beginning with achieving an audit-ready Statement of Budgetary Resources by September 30, 2014, as mandated. Given these concerns, we continue to believe that DOD could improve its risk management processes by designing and implementing department-level policies and detailed procedures that reflect the five guiding principles of effective risk management, as we recommended.

DOD also provided one general comment, suggesting that we delete reference to our prior reports on our reviews of the Navy's Civilian Pay and Air Force's Military Equipment audit readiness efforts, in which we identified significant deficiencies in the components' execution of the FIAR Guidance. Although DOD provided an update of progress made since we issued those reports, we have not reviewed those results, and in any case, we included these examples to demonstrate the difficulties encountered by the components in successfully executing the FIAR Guidance effectively and consistently. The examples also show that the components' initial attempts to assert audit readiness may not be successful and that additional time and mitigating actions may be needed to address components' deficiencies in implementing the FIAR Guidance.

As agreed with your offices, unless you publicly announce the contents of this report earlier, we plan no further distribution until 30 days from the report date. At that time, we will send copies to the appropriate congressional committees, Secretary of Defense, and other interested parties. In addition, the report will be available at no charge on the GAO website at http://www.gao.gov.

If you or your staff have any questions concerning this report, please contact me at (202) 512-9869 or khana@gao.gov. Contact points for our Offices of Congressional Relations and Public Affairs may be found on the last page of this report. GAO staff members who made key contributions to this report are listed in appendix II.

Asif A. Khan
Director
Financial Management and Assurance

Appendix I: Comments from the Department of Defense

UNDER SECRETARY OF DEFENSE
1100 DEFENSE PENTAGON
WASHINGTON, DC 20301-1100

JUN 2 7 2013

COMPTROLLER

Mr. Asif Khan
Director, Financial Management and Assurance
Government Accountability Office
441 G Street, NW
Washington, DC 20548

Dear Mr. Khan:

Thank you for the opportunity to respond to Government Accountability Office (GAO) draft report GAO-13-123, "Ineffective Risk Management Could Impair Progress toward Audit-Ready Financial Statements." In this draft report, the GAO recognizes that the Department of Defense (DoD) has acted to manage department-level risks associated with preparing auditable financial statements through the Financial Improvement and Audit Readiness (FIAR) Plan. However, the draft report goes on to assert that these actions were not fully in accordance with widely recognized guiding principles for effective risk management. The GAO also plans to report that the enterprise-wide risks the Department identified were not comprehensive or sufficiently analyzed.

Pursuant to these findings, the GAO recommends that the DoD develop and implement department-level risk management policies and detailed procedures for the FIAR Initiative. Further, GAO recommends that DoD consider and incorporate, as appropriate, the Navy and Defense Logistics Agency risk management practices in department-level policies and procedures.

It is true that the Department does not have a written risk management policy specifically related to FIAR. However, we do not concur with the GAO's assessment of the Department's overall risk management of the FIAR Initiative. All common risk management activities are occurring, including identification, evaluation, remediation, and monitoring of enterprise-wide risk for the FIAR Initiative. These ongoing activities are effectively managing risk. Embedded risk management processes and activities were designed into the FIAR Initiative, including its governance structure, strategy, policies, planning, management, and reporting. Top management uses those tools to identify potential problems that may adversely impact FIAR success, and to allocate resources to address these problems. GAO previously reviewed the FIAR Guidance and reported it as reasonable to enable the department to identify and address its financial management weaknesses and thereby achieve auditability. The FIAR Guidance establishes roles and responsibilities for overall FIAR effort program management, and risk management is a component of program management.

We will take steps to improve the documentation related to FIAR risk management activities and reinforce the importance of more detailed risk management activity that logically should be taking place within each DoD element that is executing its own detailed FIAR plan.

Beginning with the next FIAR Governance Board meeting, we will reinstate the DoD Probability
and Impact Matrix for Risk Analysis for the FIAR Initiative, depicted on page 27 of the GAO
draft report. In addition, we are re-evaluating all metrics used to monitor progress and risk in
attaining audit readiness to ensure continued utility and to develop new measures, as appropriate.

We appreciate the GAO's recognition of the risk management structure at the DoD
component level, such as those developed by the Navy and Defense Logistics Agency. Risk
management is a Department-wide effort. The FIAR Directorate provides a high-level
framework for enterprise risk, while components manage the unique risks and challenges that
impact their specific efforts to achieve auditable, component financial statements.

Enclosed is a more detailed response to the draft report for your consideration. Should
you need further information, my point of contact for this matter is Ms. Carol S. Phillips.
Ms. Phillips may be reached at (571) 256-2663 or carol.phillips@osd.mil.

Sincerely,

Robert F. Hale

Enclosure:
As stated

2

Department of Defense (DoD) Response to
Government Accountability Office (GAO) Draft Report Dated May 2013
GAO-13-123 (Engagement Code 197108)

"INEFFECTIVE RISK MANAGEMENT COULD IMPAIR PROGRESS
TOWARD AUDIT-READY FINANCIAL STATEMENTS"

GAO RECOMMENDATION

The Department should design and implement department-level policies and detailed
procedures for Financial Improvement and Audit Readiness (FIAR) Plan risk management that
incorporate the five guiding principles for effective risk management: (1) Identify risks;
(2) Analyze risks; (3) Plan for risk mitigation; (4) Implement a risk mitigation plan; and
(5) Monitor risks and mitigation plans. The Department also should consider and incorporate, as
appropriate, the Navy's and Defense Logistics Agency's risk management practices in
department-level policies and procedures.

DOD RESPONSE TO GAO RECOMMENDATION

Beyond the finding that the Department does not have a written risk management policy
specifically related to FIAR, we do not concur with the GAO's assessment of the Department's
risk management of the FIAR Initiative. All common risk management activities, including
identification, evaluation, remediation, and monitoring of enterprise-wide risk for the FIAR
Initiative, are occurring and effectively managing risk. The FIAR Initiative, including its
governance structure, strategy, policies, planning, management, and reporting, was designed with
embedded risk processes and activities to help top management identify potential problems that
may adversely impact FIAR success and to allocate resources to address these problems. The
FIAR Guidance, which GAO previously reviewed and reported as reasonable to enable the
department to identify and address its financial management weaknesses and thereby achieve
auditability, establishes roles and responsibilities for overall FIAR effort program management.
Risk management is a component of program management.

We will take steps to improve the documentation related to FIAR risk management
activities and reinforce the importance of more detailed risk management activity that logically
should be taking place within each DoD element that is executing its own detailed FIAR plans.
At the next FIAR Governance Board meeting, we will reinstate the DoD Probability and Impact
Matrix for Risk Analysis for the FIAR Initiative, which is depicted on page 27 of the GAO's
draft report. In addition, we are reevaluating all metrics used to monitor progress and risk in
attaining audit readiness to ensure continued utility and to develop new measures, as appropriate.

Enclosure

ADDITIONAL INFORMATION

We appreciate the opportunity to provide information, not reflected in the GAO's draft report, on the FIAR Initiative's enterprise-wide risk management activities and processes.

A. Overview, FIAR Risk Management Activities and Processes

Section VII of the FIAR Plan Status Report, issued in May 2012, provides a high-level overview of the FIAR Initiative enterprise-wide risk assessment activities and processes. The Department identified and reported six, enterprise-wide risk categories and general mitigation measures, which DoD Components further define and tailor to support their individual execution plans. These six risk categories include:

- Lack of DoD-wide Commitment

- Insufficient Accountability

- Poor Scope and Requirements

- Unqualified or Inexperienced Personnel

- Insufficient Funding

- Information System Control Weaknesses

Some of the activities we use to continuously identify, evaluate, communicate, mitigate, and monitor enterprise-wide risk associated with the FIAR Initiative include:

- The FIAR Governance structure: FIAR Committee/Subcommittee and FIAR Other Defense Organizations Committee/Subcommittee meetings are held monthly, and the FIAR Governance Board meets quarterly. Representatives from both the functional and financial management community are members of these committees. These meetings include discussion of FIAR goals, milestones, best practices, lessons learned, and the likelihood of successful outcomes. Action items are identified, researched and evaluated, and tracked to ensure timely resolution.

- The Chief Financial Officer and Deputy Chief Financial Officer each separately host weekly meetings with DoD Component senior leaders to discuss progress and risks to success. Also, the FIAR Director/Assistant FIAR Director meets bi-weekly with Military Department and DFAS Audit Readiness senior executives to identify and discuss risk.

- Each Military Department conducts regularly scheduled meetings and participates in other forums (e.g., Army Quarterly In-Process Reviews, annual

2

Navy Financial Improvement Plan (FIP) Conference, Air Force Audit Readiness Summit), that are attended by command representatives, where audit readiness lessons learned are presented and shared.

- Lessons learned – both successes and challenges – and best practices are communicated in various ways, such as in FIAR Governance committee meetings, working groups, online portals, newsletters, In-Process Reviews, conferences, town hall meetings, audits, etc.

- Risks are analyzed and prioritized for impact – significance and likelihood – and presented to the FIAR Governance committees.

- The semi-annual FIAR Plan Status Report includes signed messages from the Military Department Chief Management Officers of the Military Departments. The messages highlight progress and challenges, and indicate if their departments are on track to achieve audit readiness by September 30, 2017.

- Experienced auditors evaluate and report on the Component's FIPs, submitted on a monthly/bi-monthly basis, which reflect DoD Component progress and challenges, including material weaknesses and corrective actions. The FIP evaluations provide the Office of the Under Secretary of Defense (Comptroller) (OUSD(C)) with an improved understanding of the Components' plans and progress and identify risks to their successful completion of FIAR goals and milestones.

- The FIAR staff reviews the Components' annual statement of assurance and reported material weaknesses over internal controls for financial reporting and financial systems, ensuring corrective action plans are in place and that Department-level weaknesses are identified for correction.

The FIAR Directorate defined a response to each of the six enterprise-wide risk factors and implemented several activities to reduce the probability and/or impact of these risks. The FIAR Directorate also developed metrics as tools to help monitor progress in these areas. As previously stated, the FIAR Directorate currently is reevaluating all metrics used to monitor FIAR progress and risk in attaining audit readiness to ensure continued utility and to develop new measures, as appropriate.

B. Service Providers and Financial Documentation

The GAO reports that it identified two additional major risks that the Department failed to identify, specifically, risk related to (1) the Component's reliance on Service Providers for significant aspects of their financial operations, such as processing and recording financial transactions; and (2) the lack of a department-wide effort to follow documentation retention standards to ensure that required audit support can be provided to auditors.

3

Although not labeled as "risks," the FIAR Directorate identified and planned actions
to address these challenges early on in the FIAR effort.

1. Service Provider: The Department identified the critical role of the Service
   Providers during the early stages of planning for audit readiness, and
   accordingly, developed an overall FIAR strategy with specific activities and
   milestones to ensure success in this area. The FIAR Guidance established the
   roadmap for Service Providers and Reporting Entities to evaluate the
   end-to-end processes, identify risks, develop common control objectives, and
   ensure controls are designed to mitigate those risks. To monitor progress and
   facilitate communication and implementation of the FIAR Guidance:

   - The FIAR Directorate established a separate Service Provider Working
     Group to provide a forum and facilitate communication between the
     Reporting Entities and Service Providers. In these sessions, progress
     is closely monitored, issues and challenges are discussed, and roles
     and responsibilities are defined.

   - The FIAR governance bodies monitor the progress of Service
     Providers and address unresolved issues.

   - The FIAR Directorate led a series of end-to-end working groups for
     material assessable units, with both the Service Provider and Reporting
     Entities participating, to define roles and responsibilities and key control
     activities to ensure all risks and control objectives are addressed.

   - The FIAR Directorate has conducted several mock audits of the
     Service Providers' key assessable units to include assessment of
     business processes and systems that affect the financial statements.
     The FIAR Directorate continues to work very closely with the Service
     Providers to address any deficiencies found through the mock audits,
     from designing the corrective actions to assessment of effectiveness.

   - The FIAR Directorate also requires that Service Providers undergo a
     Statement on Standards for Attestation Engagements (SSAE) 16
     examination in Fiscal Year (FY) 2014, the year before the mandated
     audit of the Statement of Budgetary Resources (SBR), to allow
     sufficient time to implement corrective actions, as necessary.

2. Supporting documentation. Early on, the Department identified and addressed
   the challenges related to document retention as a critical factor in achieving an
   unqualified audit opinion. For example:

   - The FIAR Guidance lists key supporting documentation (KSD) needed
     for each line item and also provides specific examples for some of the

4

key assessable units. Further, the Guidance identifies document management as a necessary infrastructure for Reporting Entities undergoing first year audits.

- The FIAR governance bodies are identifying the requirements and monitoring the planning process for necessary audit infrastructure to include document management.

- As reflected in the FIAR Plan Status Report issued in November 2010, the FIAR Directorate monitors and tracks the Components' progress in assessing KSD to achieve end-state auditability and a strong internal control program.

- The FIAR Directorate continues to share lessons and specific examples learned through mock audits or other examinations with the Components.

In addition to the above actions, the FIAR Directorate coordinated and is finalizing a Department-wide policy update to the DoD Financial Management Regulation, Volume 1, Chapter 9, "Financial Records Retention." The update addresses documentation types and retention periods to further communicate supporting documentation and retention requirements. On June 20, 2013, we provided the GAO with a copy of the latest draft policy on financial records retention, currently under review by the Office of General Counsel and planned for DoD-wide issuance in July 2013.

C. Risk Mitigation Actions

The GAO reports that the Department's risk mitigation actions are not detailed or sufficient and cites two examples: (1) Information Systems Control Weaknesses, citing ERP schedule slippages and cost over-runs; and (2) Non-specific actions related to the risk of unqualified or inexperienced personnel.

In our opinion, the FIAR Initiative's risk mitigation actions are effective and reasonable. The following information provides specific risk mitigation actions related to the two examples cited in the GAO's draft report.

1. Information Systems Control Weaknesses. As reported in the May 2012 FIAR Plan Status Report, the Department recognized the ability of its business and financial systems to record and report accurate and auditable financial information as one of the six most challenging enterprise-wide risks to achieving audit readiness. Regardless of whether a Component is relying on a legacy system environment or a mixed environment of ERP and legacy systems, the effectiveness of application and general controls is critical to audit readiness. The risk of weak system controls is exacerbated by the

5

concurrent, ongoing, extensive modernization of the Department's hundreds of business and financial systems in the Military Departments and most Defense agencies.

The FIAR Directorate continues to mitigate and monitor the risk associated with information system control weaknesses. For example:

- FIAR Guidance requires that Reporting Entities identify and ensure audit readiness activities are in place for those systems, whether owned and managed by the Reporting Entity or owned and managed by an external DoD organization, that are relevant to the scope of individual assessable unit assertions.

- The FIAR Directorate reviews the audit readiness deliverables for these systems and provides feedback on the completeness of the population of identified systems, relative risk/priority of systems, controls documentation, testing results, and planned corrective actions. The same FISCAM-based FIAR deliverables are required for those systems managed by service provider organizations or those systems managed by the reporting entities.

- The FIAR Directorate also has undertaken an initiative to compile and evaluate systems' control testing deficiencies identified during financial statement audits, SSAE 16 examinations, assertion examinations, and audit readiness testing performed by the reporting entities and service providers.

- For those systems that have a DoD-wide audit readiness impact, the FIAR Directorate has encouraged the relevant Service Providers to pursue an SSAE 16 (Service Organization Controls 1) examination opinion in FY 2014, one year earlier than required, to allow time to remediate issues before the first SBR audits, which are scheduled to begin in FY 2015.

- The FIAR Directorate monitors and reports the status of the SSAE 16 financial systems' readiness efforts during Service Provider Working Group meetings and FIAR meetings with the reporting entities.

In addition, and concurrent with efforts to monitor the audit readiness status of existing financial information systems, the FIAR Directorate participates in additional initiatives to ensure audit readiness considerations are being addressed by new system programs:

- The OUSD(C) Business Integration Office and FIAR Directorate review and provide input related to systems' audit readiness and

6

interoperability to the Deputy Chief Management Officer's systems
Investment Decision Memorandum, Acquisition Decision
Memorandum, and Defense Acquisition Executive Summary reviews:

- o Program Schedule

- o System Performance

- o Testing and Evaluation

- o Sustainment

- o Management

- o Interoperability / Information Assurance

- o Production

- The FIAR Directorate is collaborating with the DoD Chief Information
Officer to strengthen DoD Certification and Accreditation instructions
by aligning requirements to the FIAR Guidance and incorporating
incremental control documentation and testing requirements for
systems that have an impact on financial statement audit readiness.

- The FIAR Directorate is assisting the Office of the Director,
Operations, Testing, and Evaluation, in developing a series of test
plans to evaluate Federal Financial Management Information Act
compliance and financial statement audit readiness at key milestones
in the system development lifecycle.

2. Unqualified or Inexperienced personnel. The GAO reports that actions to
mitigate the risk associated with unqualified or inexperienced financial
personnel are insufficiently detailed, making it difficult to determine if the
mitigation actions are sufficient. Specifically, the GAO reports that the
mitigation plans:

- Do not reflect the Department's actions to comply with the National
Defense Authorization Act (NDAA) for Fiscal Year 2010
(Public Law 111-84), Section 1108(a), which, in part, requires the
Department (the Under Secretary of Defense for Personnel and
Readiness in consultation with the Under Secretary of Defense for
Acquisition, Technology, and Logistics) to prepare a strategic
workforce plan (SWP) to shape and improve the civilian employee
workforce of the Department of Defense, and conduct a gap analysis in

7

the existing or projected civilian employee workforce to ensure DoD has continued access to the critical skills and competencies;

- Do not address how many certified public accountants DoD plans to hire;

- Do not address the relevant criteria to determine who should attend FIAR training;

- Do not address how the DoD financial management certification program will coincide with the current mandatory training; and

- Do not address how or which existing training and education programs will be modified, as well as timeframes, intent, and who will attend these classes.

3. DoD Response

The Department does not agree that its actions to mitigate the risk associated with unqualified or inexperienced financial personnel are insufficiently detailed, and provides the following information for GAO consideration.

Regarding the Department's compliance with the NDAA for FY 2010, Section 1108(a), the Office of the Under Secretary of Defense for Personnel and Readiness (OUSD(P&R)) plans to deliver the FY 2013-2018 SWP, which includes a chapter on the financial management (FM) community, to Congress on September 30, 2013. The OUSD(P&R) is deploying an enterprise-level competency assessment tool, the Defense Competency Assessment Tool (DCAT), which will be used by the FM workforce to assess competency gaps. The DCAT, which will provide the capability of a consistent methodology across the Department when assessing gaps, is scheduled to deploy in FY 2014; the FM workforce is scheduled to participate in the DCAT pilot program. The OUSD(C) expects a fully mature DCAT to provide FM leadership with workforce data that will assist in strategic and operational assessments of critical competency gaps of the current FM workforce; however, the initial version of DCAT will have limited capability.

Implementation of the DoD FM Certification Program, a three-tiered program, began in June 2013 and will be at full implementation by July 2014. The DoD FM Certification Program supports the professional development of the FM workforce and provides a framework for a standard body of knowledge across the FM workforce. The foundational framework for the Program is the set of 23 enterprise-wide FM competencies, associated proficiency levels, and selected leadership competencies. The Program will ensure that the FM workforce has the requisite FM knowledge, skills, and abilities to perform

8

effectively in all FM career series and will contribute to closing competency
gaps in FM and will also identify leadership training requirements. The
requirements at each certification level of the FM Certification Program for
FM and leadership competencies were derived from a senior working group of
DoD FM leaders. Additionally, specific training in audit readiness is required
for each member of the FM workforce, based on certification level. Web-based
training courses in audit readiness have been directly developed from the
existing instructor-led training courses offered by the FIAR Directorate.

The policy for the DoD FM Certification Program, Directive-Type
Memorandum (DTM) 13-004, was signed on March 22, 2013, and work is
progressing on the DoD Instruction. The policy establishes a certification
program management structure to provide governance and ensures that the
Program objectives are achieved, as well as delineating responsibilities and
prescribing procedures. The DTM defines the FM workforce as all DoD
military and civilian personnel who perform FM work and are assigned to FM
positions. FM positions are those civilians in the 05XX series, military in FM
occupational specialties, and others designated by DoD Components, as
appropriate. The DTM provides Components the authority to include
non-financial management personnel in the DoD FM Certification Program.

The Program also provides a mechanism to ensure that the FM community is
meeting critical training requirements in areas such as auditable financial
statements, fiscal law, and decision analytics to better assist commanders and
managers in using information to make decisions. The DoD FM Certification
Program is a long-term workforce development initiative. FM workforce
members have two years to achieve initial certification and are required to
maintain certification for the entire duration of their FM career. A DoD FM
Certification Program Pilot was conducted July 2012 through March 2013.
The Pilot included 650 members of the FM community from 13 different
organizations and focused on the use of the DoD FM Learning Management
System.

The OUSD(C) identified and has taken action to mitigate and monitor the
enterprise-wide risk associated with unqualified or inexperienced personnel.
OUSD(C) recognized that most individuals have never experienced the
preparation for or conduct of a financial statement audit. To mitigate this
problem and risk to success, the Department has taken the following actions:

- Hiring independent public accounting firms to help the Department
  prepare for audit;

- The FIAR Directorate developed eight separate FIAR training courses,
  six of which are certified by the National Association of State Boards

9

of Accountancy, and provides this training on a DoD-wide basis to
both functional and financial DoD employees;

- Conducting limited-scope examinations and audits of portions of the
financial statements that provide firsthand experience to prepare for
and support an audit; and

- Taken steps to ensure adequate funds are available to the Components
for FIAR activity, despite significant Department-wide budget
reductions. DoD has included a new program element specifically for
FIAR funds within the Future Years Defense Program and annual
budget process to closely monitor the use of funds.

The DoD Components are responsible for identifying, evaluating, mitigating,
monitoring, and communicating risks associated with implementing audit
readiness in their organization. Decisions related to how many CPAs should
be hired, who should attend FIAR training, etc., are made at the Component or
local level based on an assessment of their own unique challenges.

E. General Comments

We suggest the GAO delete the following information, reported on page 3 of the draft
report:

For example, our review of the Navy's Civilian Pay and Air Force's
Military Equipment audit readiness efforts identified significant
deficiencies in the components' execution of the FIAR guidance, resulting
in insufficient testing and unsupported conclusions.

On June 7, 2012, the DoD Office of Inspector General opined that the Air Force's
assertion of audit readiness for the existence, completeness, and rights of its aircraft,
satellites, cruise missiles, and aerial targets/drones, as of December 31, 2011, and
intercontinental ballistic missiles, as of January 31, 2012, is fairly stated in all
material respects.[1] On March 13, 2013, Grant Thornton, an independent audit firm,
opined that the Navy's assertion on the audit readiness of Civilian Pay is fairly stated
in all material respects.[2]

---

[1] DoD Office of Inspector General report DODIG-2012-100, "Independent Auditor's Report on the Examination of
the Existence, Completeness, and Rights of the Department of the Air Force's Aircraft, Intercontinental Ballistic
Missiles, Satellites, Cruise Missiles, and Aerial Targets/Drones," June 7, 2012
[2] Grant Thornton, LLP, Report of Independent Certified Public Accountants on Management's Assertion of Audit
Readiness, Audit Readiness Validation Examination of the Department of Navy Civilian Payroll assessable unit,
March 13, 2013

10

Appendix II: GAO Contact and Staff Acknowledgments

GAO Contact	Asif A. Khan, (202) 512-9869 or khana@gao.gov
Staff Acknowledgments	In addition to the contact named above, Cindy Brown Barnes (Assistant Director), Francine DelVecchio, Kristi Karls, and Carroll M. (CJ) Warfield, Auditor-in-Charge, made key contributions to this report. Also contributing to this report were Cynthia Jackson, Maxine Hattery, and Jason Kirwan.